ENGLISH
Pupil Book 3

Tom Watt
with
Gillian Howell

Rising Stars UK Ltd, 22 Grafton Street, London W1S 4EX

www.risingstars-uk.com

Published 2008
Text, design and layout © Rising Stars UK Ltd.

Story author: Tom Watt
Educational author: Gillian Howell
Publisher: Gill Budgell
Cover design: Burville-Riley Partnership
Design and project management: Cambridge Publishing Management
Editorial: Clare Robertson
Illustrations: David Woodroffe
Photographs: Getty Images

British Library Cataloguing in Publication Data.
A CIP record for this book is available from the British Library.

ISBN: 978-1-84680-300-0

Printed by: Craftprint International Ltd, Singapore

Rising Stars would like to thank Alan Sefton and Scott Cohen of Football in the Community for Arsenal Football Club for their help and support.

Contents

Kick-Off!

• Issue 35

Ones To Watch

3. Stuart Dolan (Shelby Town)

We all love a player who comes up through the ranks. Even better if he's a fan of your club. In our series on young players to watch out for next season, here's a rising star Shelby Town fans are proud of on both counts!

Stuart Dolan got taken to watch Shelby Town for the first time when he was four. Now he's the local hero who helped save the club from relegation last season. Stuart told **Kick-Off!** he loves life at Manor Park:

'My grandad was always a Town supporter and I got it from him, I suppose. I've been training at the club since I was a schoolboy. Getting my chance last season was a dream come true. If Dotun Odegbame hadn't got injured, I'd still be on the subs' bench now. But Mick Diamond believed in me and the fans have been fantastic.'

That's not surprising, Stuart! The speedy striker came in and scored vital goals. In fact, his winner against Spurs made him the youngest goalscorer in Shelby Town history. It was a night Stuart will never forget:

'I knew I had a chance of playing but it wasn't until the game kicked off that I realised it was actually happening. I was playing up front for Shelby Town against one of the most famous teams in England!'

There were plenty of rumours this summer linking Stuart with a big-money move away from Manor Park. Newcastle, Everton and Manchester City were all said to be interested. Stuart says he's happy where he is:

'I don't believe everything I read in the papers! That's another thing I got from my grandad! Anyway, I don't want to play for anybody else. Shelby Town are in the Premier League and they're my club. I know everyone here, and the boss has got a real family atmosphere going. Shelby is where I belong!'

And we bet Town fans are happy to hear it, Stuart! Watch out for the teenage striker who's making a name for himself at Manor Park. **Kick-Off!** wouldn't be surprised to see Stuart Dolan named in one of Stuart Pearce's England under-21 squads before the end of the season!

Shelby STFC **Town**

Stuart Dolan
Youth Team

14

Team Talk:
🛡 Talk about how Stuart and his family would feel if he became part of the England under-21 squad.
🛡 What would you tell a reporter about yourself for a magazine article?

Skills Practice 1

Put the missing punctuation into these sentences.

a) Three clubs are interested in Stuart Dolan Newcastle Everton and Manchester City

b) I don't believe everything I read in the papers said Stuart

c) If Dotun Odegbame hadnt been injured Stuart wouldnt have played

d) Stuart his mum and his grandad are all Shelby Town fans

Skills Practice 2

Replace the / in these statements with the verb phrase *said Stuart* and add correct punctuation.

a) My grandad was always a Town supporter / and I got it from him I suppose

b) If Dotun Odegbame hadn't got injured / I'd still be on the subs' bench now

c) Shelby Town are in the Premier League / and they're my club

Rewrite this conversation using correct punctuation.

How do you rate Manchester City's chances he asked now that they have dropped four points behind the leaders
We're still in with a chance I answered but we're taking nothing for granted

Game On

Answer these questions with full sentences.

1. Why is Stuart described as 'a local hero'?
2. Describe two ways in which Stuart was influenced by his grandad.
3. What part did Dotun Odegbame play in Stuart's success?
4. What happened on the night that Stuart will never forget?
5. Write a sentence describing how Stuart might feel if another club had bought him.

Match-day programme Shelby Town v Aston Villa, August 12, Kick-off 3.00

August 12

The Diamond vision

First of all, welcome to the staff, players and supporters of today's visitors, Aston Villa. They're a club with a great history and a bright future. I'm sure we'll get a good game against them today.

I also want to welcome you all to a new season at Manor Park. Thanks to the efforts of the players last season, this will be our second in the Premier League. Hopefully, we won't be fighting another relegation battle this time around!

I know some supporters are worried that we haven't spent more money in the transfer market over the summer. That was my decision. As you probably know, I spent most of my career in the lower divisions as a player. The injury that ended my playing career early made me think a lot about what I wanted to achieve as a coach and a manager.

I will always be grateful to Mr Carstairs for giving me the opportunity to get a start in management. It's not gone too badly so far, has it? Promotions, a Carling Cup Final and a first-ever season for us in the Premier League. I hope you've enjoyed the adventure as much as I have!

Shelby Town don't have the financial resources to compete against the big boys when it comes to signing top players. We have to take a different route: taking a chance with lads from the Football League and developing our own players here at the Academy.

I think we've got a really professional team here, on and off the pitch. Our team spirit and togetherness are a big plus. In areas where we don't need to spend a lot of money, such as scouting, player development, sports science and preparation for games, I expect us to be as good as anybody in the Premier League.

My philosophy is that we'll succeed or fail as a family. We're all in this together and that includes you, the supporters. Thanks for your loyalty. Stick with us: whatever else, we'll give it our best shot again!

Up the Town! *Mick Diamond*

Shelby STFC **Town**

Mick Diamond
Manager

Team Talk: 🛡 Why don't Shelby Town have the financial resources to buy big-name players?
🛡 How does the team you play for find new players?

Skills Practice 1

Put the missing commas in these sentences.

a) Welcome to the staff players and supporters of today's visitors.

b) So far we have experienced promotions a Carling Cup Final and a first-ever season for us in the Premier League.

c) In his long career Mick Diamond has been a player a coach and a manager.

Manager's Message
You do not need a comma before *and* in these sentences.

Game On

Skills Practice 2

The first paragraph in the text begins with *First of all*. Choose a connective from the following list that could be used to begin each of the remaining paragraphs.

a) In addition   **d)** Moreover

b) Furthermore   **e)** However

c) Nevertheless   **f)** Finally

Choose a connective word or phrase to begin this sentence.

_____ we are at the top of the table there are still several matches to be played.

Answer these questions with full sentences.

1. How many seasons have Shelby Town played in the Premier League?

2. Who took the decision about how much to spend in the transfer market?

3. Why would fans worry that Shelby Town haven't spent more money on transfers?

4. What does Mick Diamond mean when he says they have a professional team 'off the pitch'?

5. Describe two of Mick Diamond's purposes in writing this article.

Shelby STFC Town

Ernest Carstairs
Chairman

Who's Who

Carstairs, Ernest; OBE
Football club chairman and business entrepreneur

Date of birth: 13 Jan. 1947

Place of birth: Hounsfield, Notts, UK

Family: s. of Geoffrey K. Carstairs and Hilda Smith Carstairs; m. Delia Westport Sutton 1977; one s. Geoffrey, one d. Emilia

Education: Osborne School, Shelby and London School of Economics

Career: After graduating from LSE, joined Dillon & Partners as business analyst. Left to set up chain of fish restaurants in Scotland and North East of England. Expanded into hotel trade across UK: established Carstairs Hotel and Leisure PLC. Sold business in 1991, retained as non-executive director. Currently has controlling interest in retail packaging business, BOIT, based in Paris, France. Since 1994, Chairman of Shelby Town FC. Bought club outright in 1997. Has overseen rise of club to English Premier League.

Honours and awards: BSc, London School of Economics 1968; Northern Eye Restaurateur of the Year 1979; Hotel Society Special Award 1988; Chairman, Shelby and District Round Table 1991 to date; Freeman of Shelby 1996; Honneur d'Industrie 1999; Chairman, Football League Commercial Committee 2001–2004; Chair, Leeside Youth and Industry Alliance 2002 to date; Midlands Man of the Year 2006; OBE Services to Industry and the Community 2006; Hon. President, Shelby Town Supporters Club

Publications: Silver Service: Adventures in the Catering Trade (1990); Man and Boy (Memoir) (2001)

Leisure interests: Walking, fishing, choral music, football

Contact details: c/o Shelby Town FC, Manor Park, Shelby, Leeside, UK
BOIT, 17 Rue de Armentières, Paris, France

Links: Shelby Town: *shelby.premiumtv.co.uk* BOIT Packaging: *boit.carstairs.fr*

Team Talk: Why do some people have an entry in *Who's Who*?
What would your *Who's Who* entry say?

Skills Practice 1

Write these singular nouns as plurals.

a) chairman
b) business
c) community
d) league
e) family
f) trade

Skills Practice 2

Write these noun phrases as plurals.

a) school of economics
b) man and boy
c) freeman of Shelby

Change the nouns in this sentence into plural nouns.

The first match is always challenging as an indicator of the strength and weakness of the team.

Manager's Message
What else do you need to change in order to make sense of the sentences?

Game On

Answer these questions with full sentences.

1. What are the names of Ernest Carstairs' mother and father?
2. What was Ernest Carstairs' first job after he graduated?
3. Give two examples that show how successful Carstairs' restaurant business was.
4. How does Carstairs spend his spare time?
5. How do you think Carstairs has contributed to community life in Shelby?

Shelby Town FC

August 29

Dear Parent,

I'm delighted that you have agreed for your son to start training with our schoolboys on Monday and Friday evenings. His safety, welfare and academic progress are all very important to us. We will give him the best football education we can, and hope to help with any other issues that you bring to our attention. Feel free to ring me or call in at the club at any time.

As Academy Director here at Manor Park, I should introduce myself. I have been in the post for nearly five years now. I believe that in the time I've been in the job we have established a sound, professional organisation at the club. We pride ourselves on the way we develop young players and believe that they are the future for Town.

I have always loved and played football. In my twenties, I played semi-professionally for a number of clubs in the South East, such as Leatherhead, and Epsom and Ewell. Back in the 1960s, the non-league game was flourishing and I enjoyed every minute of my time as a player. At the same time, I had a full-time career as a secondary school teacher. I always made sure I had time to run school football teams outside of school hours!

My involvement with the professional game began fifteen years ago. I was asked to scout and do schools liaison for Brentford, Oxford United and then Reading. The opportunity to move north to Leeside and work with Shelby Town full-time came out of the blue. I had all the necessary qualifications and was introduced to the Town Chairman, Mr Carstairs, through a mutual friend. The rest, as they say, is history!

Shelby Town

Derek Hardaker
Academy Director

The role of Academy Director is a very satisfying one. It's also a great challenge. As I say, we believe your son may turn out to be vital to Shelby Town's future. Best of luck to him and the boys he'll be training with. I'm sure he'll enjoy every minute of it!

Yours faithfully,

Derek Hardaker

Derek Hardaker, Academy Director, Shelby Town FC

Shelby Town FC

Team Talk:
🛡 Look at the third paragraph. What does it tell you about Derek Hardaker's personality?
🛡 How do you think out-of-school-hours football would benefit pupils?

Skills Practice 1

Rewrite these sentences by moving the underlined clause.

a) <u>When you join the Academy</u> we will take care of your academic studies.

b) I believe <u>in the time I've been in the job</u> that we have established a sound, professional organisation.

c) <u>I enjoyed every minute of my time</u> as a player when the non-league game was flourishing.

d) Make sure your son brings the letter <u>when he first comes to the Academy</u>.

Skills Practice 2

Underline the main clause in this sentence.

When he wrote the letter to parents, rather than outlining a bold vision of the future, the manager concentrated on the little things such as the confidence of the boys, their work rate and their commitment to football.

Manager's Message
Remember correct punctuation and capital letters.

Game On

Answer these questions with full sentences.

1. How many times does training take place each week?
2. How old was Derek Hardaker when he played semi-professional football?
3. What does Derek Hardaker mean when he says that young players are the 'future for Town'?
4. What does the saying 'out of the blue' mean?
5. Write a sentence to describe the overall purpose of this letter.

Shelby **STFC** Town

Raphael MacDonald
Under-13s Team

Raphael MacDonald

Year 8

What a weekend!

I look forward to every weekend. I am a schoolboy footballer at Shelby Town FC and train with the under-13s every Monday and Friday evening. We have games, sometimes on a Saturday morning or sometimes on Sunday. I love the training but I enjoy the games even more.

Training is at 5pm on Monday and 6pm on Friday, for two hours. We have to make sure we are on time. Dad usually takes me there and he will hang around and watch and talk to the other mums and dads. When Mum comes, I think she gets bored quite quickly! She goes and has a coffee and comes back to pick me up.

In the summer we train at the training ground and during the winter we use the indoor hall. Graham Hicks is the coach who usually works with us. He always has a laugh with us. But he makes sure we are serious when we need to be listening or learning something new. We practise different things on different nights. I like it when we do one against one best, because I can try out tricks to beat my man. We always have small-sided games as well.

Mr Hardaker is the Academy Director and he is usually there too. He doesn't do so much coaching but he talks to us and to our mums and dads. He is always telling parents that they are welcome to watch and encourage us by being there. But he says that only the coaches are allowed to shout out to us! I think it took a little while for Dad to get used to that! Mr Hardaker gets us tickets for first-team games as well.

Our games at the weekend are the best time of all. We meet up at the training ground in the morning, and if we have an away game we travel together in a minibus. This Sunday we were away to Coventry City, which was quite a long ride. It was worth it, though. We won 3-1 and I scored two of the goals. We were singing so loud on the way home, Graham had to tell us to shut up because he couldn't concentrate on his driving!

Team Talk:

🛡 Find the verbs in the text. Why has Raphael used mostly present-tense verbs?

🛡 What do you most enjoy doing at the weekends?

Skills Practice 1

Change these verbs from the text into nouns, by adding a suffix.

a) enjoy
b) bore
c) laugh
d) encourage
e) concentrate

Manager's Message
Remember, changing verbs into nouns is like this: arrange/arrangement.

Skills Practice 2

Write the root word of each of these football terms.

a) Premiership
b) championship
c) midfielder
d) manager
e) relegation
f) striker
g) division
h) equaliser

Game On

Answer these questions with full sentences.

1. When do the under-13s have football matches?
2. What time does training finish on Fridays?
3. Why does Raphael like practising one-on-one best?
4. Why are coaches the only ones allowed to shout out at the boys?
5. What do you think Raphael enjoys most about the weekends?

Well, first of all, I'd like to say thanks very much for inviting me to come to Osborne School to talk about my job. I think I recognise a few of you from Saturday afternoons at Manor Park. I definitely know Raphael, over there, and Steven, who are both training with us at Shelby Town.

My name is Phil Miles and I'm the Secretary at Shelby Town. Now when I say I'm the secretary, you probably think that means I take dictation and make the coffee. Well, I've actually got another secretary – the Secretary's secretary, I suppose – who types up letters and does the filing and that sort of thing. I do make my own coffee, though!

When I started eight years ago, we were still in the old Third Division. The job has changed a bit now we're in the Premier League. It's been great being part of the rise of Shelby Town and I suppose I've learnt the new stuff as I've gone along. We didn't have any French or Nigerian players, like Pierre Vert or Dotun Odegbame back then, for a start!

So, what do I do? Well, the football club is a limited company like any other business, so there's a lot of legal stuff to take care of, like the accounts. I keep an eye on everything that affects the football club as a business, really. The interesting bit of the job is what I have to do with the players, even though that's the side of it that drives me mad sometimes as well. I have to draw up all the contracts for players, right down from the first team to the arrangements for schoolboys like Raphael and Steven.

Shelby STFC **Town**

Phil Miles
Secretary

The busiest days are when there's a game on at Manor Park. I have to set things up with everybody involved with the match. That's our caterers and stewards and turnstile operators and programme sellers, of course. But I also deal with the referee and linesmen, the police, the medical people and the club shop. And, if it's a big game, I'll make all the arrangements with the TV companies as well.

There's not much that goes on that I don't have a hand in! You'll know what interests you most about what goes on behind the scenes at Town. Why don't you fire away with some questions? Who's first?

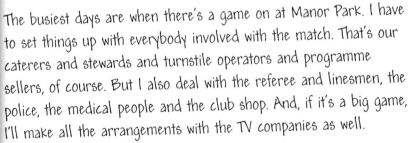

Team Talk:

🛡 Think of two questions you would ask about what happens 'behind the scenes'.

🛡 Who would you like to come and give a speech at your school, and why?

Skills Practice 1

Change these nouns into verbs.

E.g. *dictation / dictate.*

a) division
b) decision
c) creation
d) relation
e) prediction

Skills Practice 2

Which verbs in the sentences below can be turned into nouns?

a) Everton have maintained their place in the Premier League since it began.
b) Newcastle were close to being relegated when Kevin Keegan began managing them.
c) West Ham secured their Premier League place after being absent for two years.

Game On

Answer these questions with full sentences.

1. In which division did Shelby Town play when Phil Miles joined them?
2. How long has Phil Miles been at Shelby Town?
3. Think of three business aspects that the Secretary might have to deal with.
4. Why are match days the busiest for the Secretary?
5. Why do you think the job has changed?

New Message

Send Chat Attach Address Fonts Colors Save As Draft

To: Phil Miles

Cc: All ticket office staff

Subject:

Account: Nisha Doshi nishad@shelbytown.co.uk   Signature: email address

Good morning, all. Very busy day today, as we discussed yesterday! I've tried to organise a schedule for us all. Don't know how long we'll be able to stick to it! I know I can trust you all to muck in where you need to.

Angela, Tom and Andy: The tickets for the Cup game at Bristol City have arrived. We've got 4,500 to distribute. Because of the hold-up at their printers, all tickets will be sold to personal callers. There's no time to put our usual postal system in place. You could have a long day at the ticket windows! Two tickets per person. If supporters turn up with extra season tickets (friends, family, etc.), then they can buy extra tickets for them. Your first job is to sort out the queues. Try not to spend too long on the phone to people explaining the situation. But don't be rude!

Phil: Because the team had such a good December, we're getting a lot of calls about half-year season tickets. All calls about them will be put through to you today. You may need to go out into the lobby to meet supporters, too. We don't want them getting stuck in the queues for the Cup tickets! You know the details: half a season is half the full season price plus £10. If you can, get fans to pay by credit card over the phone or by cash/cheque if they come in to see you. Sooner the better! There are only another ten days of this scheme to run.

Jack: Need you to go through the postal applications for tickets for the Arsenal game on the 29th. Simple enough but you're on your own. Check dates and signatures on cheques, won't you? You wouldn't believe how many we had sent back from the bank after Everton!

I'll be around all day. I've got to take players' tickets down to the training ground and I'll take the Schoolboys' allocation for Derek Hardaker, too. **Phil:** I know you're busy but would you be able to take care of all the directors' passes and tickets for Bristol?

Anybody with a problem, find me or give me a call. Good luck!

Nisha Doshi,
Ticket Office Manager,
Shelby Town FC

Shelby STFC Town

Nisha Doshi
Ticket Office Manager

Team Talk: 🛡 Why is an email message a good way of getting information to several people at once?
🛡 How do you get tickets for your team's matches?

Skills Practice 1

Choose the correct spelling from the words in brackets for the missing word in these sentences.

a) I've tried to organise a schedule _____ us all. (*four, fore, for*)

b) Because of the hold-up at _____ printers, all tickets will be sold to personal callers. (*they're, there, their*)

c) All calls about them will be put _____ to you today. (*threw, through*)

d) Try not _____ spend _____ long on the phone. (*two, too, to*)

Skills Practice 2

Write another sentence using the underlined word to show a different meaning from its use in the text.

a) Don't know how long we'll be able to <u>stick</u> to it!

b) I know I can trust you all to <u>muck</u> in where you need to.

c) Try not to <u>spend</u> too long on the phone.

d) You wouldn't believe how many we had sent back from the <u>bank</u>.

Write down the words that have more than one meaning in this sentence.

Another three points mean Chelsea are climbing up the table and are close behind City.

Game On

Answer these questions with full sentences.

1. Who wrote the email and what is their job?
2. How many people are actually selling tickets in person?
3. Why are the tickets only being sold to personal callers?
4. Why does Nisha Doshi want people to pay for the season tickets straight away?
5. How much is Phil Miles being asked to do?

Player Report/Confidential

Player name: **Pierre Jean Vert**
Date of birth: **22 March, 1982**
Nationality: **French**
Position: **Midfield/Centre Back**
Height: **1.85m**

Shelby STFC **Town**

Pierre Jean Vert
Midfielder,
Prospective Player

Vert has been watched several times. Mick Diamond and I went to France last Sunday to watch him play for Lens against Strasbourg. Lined up in the middle of a 3-man midfield. Vert came off after 70 minutes with an ankle knock. Strasbourg scored the only goal of the game five minutes later.

Analysis

Strengths: PV is a strong, experienced defensive midfielder. Excellent reader of the game. Can also fill in as a central defender. Strong tackler. Good distribution. Danger in opposition penalty area at set plays. Doesn't over-complicate the game.

Weaknesses: PV is a good athlete but is one-paced. Does his defensive job well but doesn't have a burst that will get him into the opposition penalty area. Can be found out one-on-one against a pacy opponent (but clever enough to avoid this kind of situation).

Background Info

Grew up on an estate in Paris suburbs. Schoolboy forms with PSG but eventually signed as a youth player at Auxerre. Broke into first team as an 18-year-old, covering centre midfield and centre back. Won under-19 and under-21 caps for France but has not been included in a full squad. Moved on to Lens three years ago. A first-team regular until falling out with the coach at the end of last season. Having spoken to his agent, it is clear PV is very keen on a move to England. Has even started learning English. Last year of his contract at Lens, so price will be within our budget. Not an international, so wages should not be a problem either.

Recommendation

Phil Miles to contact Lens FC tomorrow with formal offer for transfer of PV to Shelby Town.

Brian Harris

Brian Harris (Chief Scout)

Team Talk:
🛡 What do you consider Pierre's major strength and major weakness to be?
🛡 In football, what do you consider your major strength to be?

Skills Practice 1

Rewrite each of the following incomplete sentences from the player report as a complete sentence.

a) Has even started learning English.
b) Can also fill in as a central defender.
c) Lined up in the middle of a 3-man midfield.

Skills Practice 2

Join the two clauses in each of these sentences to form complex sentences. Try to use connectives other than *and* or *but* to join the clauses.

a) Pierre has been a regular first team player. He has fallen out with the coach.
b) Pierre performed well against Strasbourg. He came off after 70 minutes.
c) Pierre is a strong defensive player. He only has one pace.

Underline the main clauses in the sentences you have written.

Manager's Message
A main clause will still make sense on its own. Subordinate clauses add information to the main clause.

Game On

Answer these questions with full sentences.

1. Who went to watch Pierre Vert in France against Strasbourg?
2. How old was Pierre Vert when he became a first-team player?
3. What do you understand by the phrase 'doesn't over-complicate'?
4. Why isn't Pierre a regular first-team player for Lens any more?
5. Write three reasons why Shelby Town might want to buy Pierre Vert.

Rob Mills (Presenter): Thanks, Emma. More travel in half an hour on BBC Radio Leeside. Back to our phone-in now. Remember you can call any time on 01929 700600 and be part of the show. We're talking about why there are so many foreign players in the Premier League these days. Even at our own club, little Shelby Town. We're joined on the line now by the man who's got the job of spotting talent for us, Chief Scout Brian Harris. Good evening, Brian.

Brian Harris: Good evening, Rob. I'm not sure it's 'little Shelby Town', by the way. We're competing at the top level now, aren't we? On and off the pitch.

Rob: Absolutely, Brian. It just seems strange to have players from all over the world finding their way here. The football world's changed since you were a player, hasn't it?

Brian: Very much so. I played in the lower divisions with Mansfield and Crewe. Our idea of a 'foreign' player was a lad from Ireland or Wales back in the '70s! And when I first started in scouting here at Town, the furthest we ever went was to Scotland!

Rob: So, why has it all changed, Brian?

Brian: Oh, all sorts of reasons. Not really my job to ask why. I just have to get on with it. What hasn't changed is that we have to get value for money for the football club. We're very keen to develop our own young players, lads who've grown up around Leeside. But if you're talking about improving the first-team squad, it's a different matter. I'll go and watch players in Portugal or Bulgaria or France, wherever we get a tip-off about someone.

Rob: What are you looking for?

Brian: Well, that's the same as it always has been. Good athletes with a bit of skill and the right attitude. We can't compete against the big clubs for the top, top players. We have to look for bargains. Sometimes we'll take a chance on a player from the lower divisions, but we find we get more for our money abroad these days. That's just how it is.

Rob: Fascinating talking to you, Brian. Thanks. That's Brian Harris. What do you think? Local lads or imported stars? Call me right now on 01929 700600.

Shelby STFC **Town**

Brian Harris
Chief Scout

Team Talk:

🛡 Would you prefer the team you support to have local lads or imported stars, and why?

🛡 How does your own team recruit new players?

Skills Practice 1

Write these sentences from the text as a conversation between Rob and Brian, using speech punctuation and speech verbs.

a) Good evening, Brian.
b) Good evening, Rob.
c) The football world's changed since you were a player, hasn't it?
d) When I first started in scouting here at Town, the furthest we ever went was to Scotland!
e) So, why has it all changed, Brian?
f) That's just how it is.

Skills Practice 2

Use speech verbs to join these pairs of sentences.

a) Well, that's the same as it always has been. Good athletes with a bit of skill and the right attitude.
b) I played in the lower divisions with Mansfield and Crewe. Our idea of a 'foreign' player was a lad from Ireland or Wales back in the 70s!
c) I'm not sure it's 'little Shelby Town', by the way. We're competing at the top level now, aren't we?

Game On

Answer these questions with full sentences.

1. What is the topic being discussed in the phone-in?
2. Which was the furthest country Brian travelled to when he first became a football scout?
3. Why does Brian describe improving the first-team squad as 'a different matter'?
4. Rob asks 'Why has it all changed?' Why do you think Brian answers in the way he does?
5. What comment would you make as part of the phone-in?

Match-day programme

Tales from the Training Ground

He's a man who never misses a game, home or away. He knows every little detail about every single player at the club. And, without him, Town would never be ready for kick-off. Our latest feature on the men who make Town tick focuses on Frank Kendall. Manager Mick Diamond has described him as the 'best kit man in football'.

In fact, Frank's official title is Kit Manager, but he says he's not fussy:

'Oh, I've been called a few names down the years,' he laughs, 'when I've forgotten something or been caught out by a practical joke. I wouldn't swap this job for anything, though. I love football and I love football people. Mick Diamond's one of the best. I feel like I'm part of the family.'

So what does Frank's job really involve? A bit more than washing and laying out the kit, according to the man himself:

'The number one responsibility is to make sure everything's ready for 3 o'clock on a Saturday afternoon. But, in between times, you wouldn't believe some of the stuff I get asked to do! The lads think I'm a car mechanic, a phone answering service, a security guard, a takeaway restaurant, a marriage guidance counsellor, a van driver and a dry cleaners as well!'

Frank's not complaining, though. He loves organising people as much as he loves working at Shelby Town:

'I was in the forces, you see, up until I was nearly 40,' he says, 'and that was all about being in the right place at the right time. I like a bit of order and things done properly. When I came out of the army, I didn't really know what I was going to do. But I knew Bill Barry, who did the job here before me, and he asked me to come down to help out. I've never left! And I don't plan to either!'

People describe Frank Kendall as being 'part of the furniture' at Manor Park. The last word on our kit manager goes to the boss:

'Frank's a Shelby Town institution,' says Mick Diamond, 'the kind of bloke every club needs. Once he stops moaning about the players, he's very good at his job. Which must be why they all love him! And why I do as well.'

Shelby STFC Town

Frank Kendall
Kit Manager

Team Talk: How would you describe Frank Kendall's personality?
 What do you to make sure your kit is ready before a match?

Skills Practice 1

Add the correct punctuation to these sentences.

a) The following are some of Frank's roles a car mechanic a phone answering service a security guard a takeaway restaurant a marriage guidance counsellor a van driver and a dry cleaners

b) Oh Ive been called a few names down the years he laughs when Ive forgotten something or been caught out by a practical joke

Skills Practice 2

Write five football sentences of your own that include the following punctuation marks.

a) a semicolon **;**
b) an exclamation mark **!**
c) commas to indicate items in a list **,**
d) a colon **:**
e) brackets **( )**

Put the correct punctuation into the following sentence.

The Premier League crown eluded Arsenal until 1998 two years into Arsène Wengers tenure when they did the League and FA Cup double.

Game On

Answer these questions with full sentences.

1. What does Frank Kendall do at Shelby Town?
2. What is Frank's most important responsibility?
3. How did his army service affect the way he approaches tasks?
4. Write a sentence to explain the phrase 'part of the furniture'.
5. In what way do you think Frank moans about the players?

WANTED: FOOTBALL FAN NOT AFRAID OF HARD WORK!

Shelby Town Football Club are looking for a new editor for their award-winning **Match Day Magazine**. Are you the person to deliver a Premier League programme for a Premier League club? Can you write, edit, interview, help with design and work to a constantly changing schedule? If the answer's yes, then we want to hear from you before June 30th!

Shelby Town are about to start their second season as a Premier League Club. We urgently need someone to come in and pick up what's already a successful product, selling an average of over 13,000 copies at every home game.

The successful applicant will need to demonstrate an ability to lead a team of freelance writers and photographers as well as in-house contributors. You will be responsible for producing the manager's and captain's pages for the programme, as well as writing main features from week to week. You will need to edit everything else in the programme, too: from pen pictures to youth team results, from league tables to commercial news.

Match Day Magazine is printed and published by a local company, DJ Press Express. The editor will need to liaise with them on a daily basis about photos, design and layout. All of this has to happen within very tight production and distribution deadlines.

Previous experience in publishing is absolutely essential. You should be comfortable in charge of a small, dedicated team. You don't have to be a **Shelby Town** supporter, but that might help, too!

The rewards for the successful applicant are a generous salary and bonuses based on sales of the programme and advertising revenue. You'll be working right at the heart of an ambitious but friendly Premier League club.

If you think you fit the bill, apply in writing today to: The Chief Executive, **Shelby Town FC**, Manor Park, Shelby, Leeside including a full CV, or by email to: jsaunders@shelbytown.co.uk, putting 'Programme Editor' in the subject box.

Team Talk:
- What examples of persuasive language can you find in this advert?
- Read the third paragraph. Would you enjoy doing this job? Why, or why not?

Skills Practice 1

> **Manager's Message**
> Apostrophes are used to show either possession (ownership) or omission (missing letters).

Write P for possession or O for omission next to these words with apostrophes. Some could show either.

a) answer's

b) what's

c) manager's

d) don't

e) you'll

Skills Practice 2

Put apostrophes where they are needed in these sentences.

a) The programmes published every week.

b) Its a weekly programme.

c) Its contents written by freelancers.

d) Whos applied for the job?

e) The person whose applications well written will get the job.

Put the apostrophe in the correct place in this sentence.

Both sides search for a victory was thwarted by strong defensive play.

Game On

Answer these questions with full sentences.

1. What is the title of the job being advertised?

2. How often will the successful applicant need to talk to the printer?

3. Why would it help to be a Shelby Town supporter?

4. Explain what 'bonuses based on sales and advertising revenue' means.

5. Write a sentence describing the kind of person you think will 'fit the bill'.

Midlands Business Life

Shelby STFC Town

Jane Saunders
Chief Executive

SAUNDERS TOP OF THE LEAGUE WITH TOWN

At Midlands Business Life magazine we believe success is about people. Every month we profile a business leader who's broken new ground and taken their company forward. This month, we're in the world of football. In the Premier League, there's a new face at the top table. Jane Saunders was running Leeside Personnel Services when she was head-hunted to become Chief Executive at her local club, Shelby Town. She took the chance to raise a few eyebrows in the man's world of professional football. In her own words, here's what makes Jane tick.

To be honest, before I got the job at Shelby Town I didn't know much about football. Maybe that was a good thing. When I first arrived, I looked at the whole business from top to bottom. And I learnt a lot! First of all, the Chief Exec's job at a football club isn't like the same job anywhere else. The team and the manager, the football side at Town, have to get on with it. I'm just here to help them. And they help me by winning!

On the commercial side, I thought we could do better. Maybe it was what the club needed: fresh ideas from somebody outside football. It's not like the old days, when you just let the fans in for three o'clock on Saturday and started counting the money! Income in the Premier League is huge, but so are the outgoings on wages and so on. I've tried to come up with ways to make match days more profitable: ticket schemes, a better programme, better catering, more hospitality packages. But we're also looking for ways to make money on the other six days of the week at Manor Park, too.

I've got good people working for me. I'm in the process of appointing more staff at the moment. I hope I'm getting the hang of the football business, too. I know I've fallen in love with the game, anyway! The important thing is that everybody at Manor Park works together as a team. Even now, in the Premier League, we haven't forgotten what got us here. I think my team tries a bit harder for our customers, the supporters, than the 'big' clubs do. And I know our fans are delighted with what Mick Diamond has done with *his* team!

14

Team Talk:
🛡 Do you think someone in charge of a football club ought to be a football fan? Why, or why not?
🛡 How does the team that you play for raise money?

Skills Practice 1

> **Manager's Message**
> The regular form of past-tense verbs has a suffix *-ed* as in *mend/mended*. Some verbs are not regular and use other forms.

Write the past-tense form of each of these verbs.

a) We believe

b) I am

c) We are

d) They take

e) I get

f) I look

Game On

Skills Practice 2

Write a sentence using the past-tense form of each of these verbs.

a) break

b) wake

c) think

d) win

e) get

f) fall

Change the underlined verbs into the present tense.

The fans <u>were woken up</u> when a penalty <u>was taken</u> by the visitors and <u>flew</u> into the back of the net.

Answer these questions with full sentences.

1. How often does the magazine print a profile of a business leader?

2. How did Jane Saunders make match days more profitable?

3. What was unusual about Jane Saunders' appointment?

4. Who do you think Jane Saunders means by 'her team'?

5. Describe Jane Saunders' role at Shelby Town.

August 27

Dear Mum and Dad,

How are you? It is hard to believe I have been here in England for a year now! Things have happened so quickly. My big news is that I got a phone call at the club from Nwankwo Kanu. The Nigerian national team manager has been asking him about me. He had good reports from his scouts. What would it be like to see Dotun Odegbame playing for the Super Eagles one day, eh?

It's funny to think I wasn't sure about coming here. I liked it in Lisbon with Benfica. They were a big club and I was comfortable in Portugal. I didn't even know where Shelby was. I knew my wages would be better in England but I didn't really know what to expect. Now I know I made the right decision.

Shelby STFC **Town**

Dotun Odegbame
Striker

This is the club's second season in the Premier League and I know you can watch my games on TV at home in Lagos. Shelby is a friendly town. Supporters often come up to me in the street to ask for an autograph or to say well done. But they are always polite, even the children!

The club have helped me a lot. When I was injured last season, they made sure I got the best care. They helped me find my apartment. The skipper, Dave Morgan, invited me to his house to meet his family. He is a legend here and he made me feel at home. Now I am part of the team.

The football in England is very good. We had a hard season and Shelby Town are not a big club. But every game is sold out and the fans are cheering from the first minute to the last. They have passion for their team. The matches are hard. It is very fast and you must be ready for some rough tackles. It's good you brought me up to be a strong boy!

Now the new season is starting. It was great to see you in the summer back home. I hope you will come and see me here soon. Love to everybody.

Your son,   **Dotun**

Team Talk: What is Dotun's 'big news'?
How do you think playing for your country differs from playing in the Premier League?

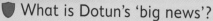

Skills Practice 1

Join these sentences from the text with a connective.

a) It is hard to believe I have been here in England for a year now _____ things have happened so quickly.

b) It's funny to think I wasn't sure about coming here _____ I liked it in Lisbon with Benfica.

c) He is a legend here and he made me feel at home _____ now I am part of the team.

d) The football in England is very good _____ we had a hard season and Shelby Town are not a big club.

Skills Practice 2

Use a connective to begin these sentences.

a) _____ I now know I made the right decision, I wasn't sure about coming here.

b) _____ Dave Morgan is a legend here, he has made me feel at home.

c) _____ it was great to see you in the summer, I hope you will come and see me here soon.

Fill in the spaces in the following sentences.

_____ the Bulgarian International made his professional debut at the age of 15, he hasn't reached the heights everyone predicted. _____ his talent is not in doubt.

Game On

Answer these questions with full sentences.

1. How long has Dotun been playing for Shelby Town?

2. For whom had Dotun been playing before he moved to Shelby?

3. Give two reasons why Dotun was unsure about moving to Shelby.

4. What part do the fans play in making Shelby a good team to play for?

5. What do you think Dotun likes most about playing for Shelby Town?

NOW SPORTS

Studio Presenter: Now Sports Sunday opens up at Manor Park this afternoon. Shelby Town versus Everton kicks off at 1.30. Already there for us: commentator Michael Taylor.

Michael Taylor: Thanks, Dougie. Yes, an absolutely perfect afternoon for football, by the look of it. Sun's shining, bit of autumn chill in the air. And the pitch here, I have to say, is looking marvellous. The man responsible for the playing surface at Shelby Town is Head Groundsman Cliff Warriner.

Cliff Warriner: Hello, Michael.

Michael: Youngest groundsman in the Premier League, Cliff. But it looks like you've got the hang of it. Bet the players here appreciate it.

Cliff: Well, Mick Diamond's not one for the lads hoofing the ball everywhere.

Michael: This is your first job, isn't it?

Cliff: Well, not exactly. After college, I was six years up at Leeside Golf Club. It was the manager who got me down here, actually. He said he wanted a pitch that played as well as the putting greens on the golf course.

Michael: So do you get the players out playing pitch and putt after training?

Cliff: I'd soon chase them off if they tried, Michael! Have you seen Dave Morgan's swing? He'd dig up a divot every time he tried to hit the ball.

Michael: So what do you have to do, apart from keeping people off the grass, Cliff?

Cliff: Well, we mow it every other day. That's after we've relaid it every summer. And then it's about feeding it, making sure it's draining OK and then marking it out for match days.

Michael: Like today. Do you worry 22 players are going to mess up all your hard work?

Cliff: Yeah! But I can't do anything about that, can I?

Michael: Well, it'll be perfect for Town and Everton later anyway. Thanks, Cliff. Join us here from one, live on Now and Now HD. Back to you, Dougie.

Shelby STFC Town

Cliff Warriner
Head Groundsman

Team Talk:
- Think of two reasons why you would enjoy being a groundsman at your club.
- How is the pitch you play on looked after?

Skills Practice 1

Rewrite these incomplete sentences, adding missing verbs.

a) An absolutely perfect afternoon for football, by the look of it.

b) Sun's shining, bit of autumn chill in the air.

c) Youngest groundsman in the Premier League, Cliff.

d) Players here appreciate it.

Skills Practice 2

Write these sentences without apostrophes so that they still make sense.

a) Mick Diamond's not one.

b) I'd soon chase them off.

c) He'd dig up a divot every time.

d) This is your first job, isn't it?

e) That's after we've relaid it.

f) I can't do anything about that.

Now try this one.

The match's over and it couldn't have been more eventful.

Game On

Answer these questions with full sentences.

1. What is the job title for a person who looks after the pitch at a football ground?

2. What was Cliff's job before he joined Shelby Town?

3. Write a sentence to explain what 'hoofing the ball everywhere' means.

4. What is Cliff's opinion of the golfing abilities of Shelby Town footballers?

5. What do you think Cliff will do immediately after the match?

SPORTS *EXTRA*

February 15th • *Shelby Gazette*

BEHIND THE SCENES AT TOWN
4. George Hufton

Shelby STFC Town

George Hufton
Match Announcer

Everybody knows the sound of his voice. Not so many know what he looks like! This picture of match announcer George Hufton should help. George himself reckons it proves what many people have said down the years: 'that I've got a great face for radio!'

George has been part of the match-day scene at Manor Park since he first read out team changes and played a few records back in 1986. He's a freelance computer programmer with a leading insurance company five days a week. His 'proper' job, though, is behind the mike during the build-up to every Shelby Town home game.

'I haven't missed one in 22 years' is George's proud boast.

George has been a Town supporter for 40 years. He says he's always worried the club will bring in a younger man – 'somebody trendy off Kiss FM or something' – but the fans won't hear of it. George enjoys the banter with the Town crowd:

'When they hear I'm the bloke reading out the team changes, they always have a laugh with me. Ask me if I pick the team too! I think Town fans quite like that I'm an old-fashioned announcer. I try and keep it simple. Saturday afternoons is about the team, not about me.'

For the club's match announcer, like the players, match day is all about preparation.

'When I was just an ordinary fan, my build-up to Saturday would start on a Thursday. Still does now! I write a rough schedule: music, dedications, birthdays, announcements and what have you. I try and build up the excitement gradually. And then there's the stuff that happens at the last minute or during a game, everything from emergency messages to the substitutions.'

George's biggest claim to fame is that the music the Town team runs out to was his idea.

'I thought of it four years ago. People were talking about us having a theme tune. I always loved old soul music. As soon as I started thinking about it, 'Green Onions' by Booker T just came into my mind! And it seems to have caught on. The supporters have even started singing along with it, haven't they?'

Team Talk: 🛡 What does 'a great face for radio' mean?
🛡 What skills do you think a good match announcer needs?

Skills Practice 1

Rewrite these sentences, adding correct speech punctuation.

a) I've got a great face for radio! laughed George

b) I try and keep it simple said George Saturday afternoons is about the team, not about me

c) I write a rough schedule he added and try and build up the excitement gradually

Skills Practice 2

Change these sentences of reported speech to direct speech.

a) George said he first read out team changes and played a few records back in 1986.

b) The reporter asked George how long he had been a Town supporter.

Change this direct speech into reported speech.

'Our reserve goalkeeper would be the number one in most other clubs,' said the Chelsea midfielder.

Game On

Answer these questions with full sentences.

1. When did George Hufton first become a match announcer?
2. What does George do for a living during the working week?
3. What does the reporter mean when he describes George's role as announcer as his 'proper' job?
4. Why does George write a rough schedule?
5. Can George plan for what happens during the match? Give a reason for your answer.

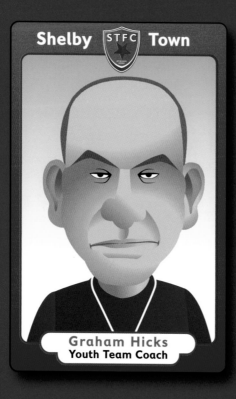

Shelby STFC **Town**

Graham Hicks
Youth Team Coach

Good morning, lads. Sit yourselves down. And if you've got a mobile there, make sure it's switched off. If I hear one ring, it's straight out the window! I think we've all met each other, haven't we? I know we haven't worked together but we'll put that right over the next two years.

My name's Graham Hicks. I'm a youth team coach now but I was a professional player for twenty years. Most of them before any of you were born! I played for this club when they were in what's now League One. But most of my career was at the top level: Southampton, Nottingham Forest – yeah, when they were a First Division club! – and Sunderland. My job now is to get you lads ready for Shelby Town's first team. Or, if you're not good enough for us, get you ready for a career somewhere else.

As new Academy scholars, you've got two years between now and a pro contract. If you mess things up for yourself, that's your problem. But if there's ever anything that you feel is holding you back, then just talk to me or Mr Hardaker about it. We'll sort it out. You deserve to make the most of this chance you've got with us. I'm going to be honest with you, boys, and I need you to be honest with me.

You'll get time with all the coaching staff here but I'll keep an eye on you, don't worry. Or maybe I mean you *should* worry! We've got Niall, the new fitness and sports science man, to keep you fit. What we're going to be doing together is learning the game, all right? Football's simple: control the ball, pass it to your mate. Make the right decisions. That's what we're about here. If you love football and work hard, we're going to enjoy ourselves, I promise.

Thanks for listening. Better get used to doing that when I'm talking! You can go and pick up your kit now. Frank Kendall's expecting you. Don't ever keep him waiting! I'll see you out on the pitches at quarter past ten. Off you go!

Team Talk:
- What might you be thinking and feeling if you were in the audience?
- Describe a speech you remember from when you started something new, e.g. a class, school or club.

Skills Practice 1

Manager's Message
Homonyms are words that are spelt and pronounced the same but have different meanings when used in different contexts.

Write two meanings for these words, one in a football context and one in a different context.

a) mobile   **d)** back

b) ring   **e)** pick

c) club   **f)** pitch

Skills Practice 2

Write two sentences for these words that use them in a) a football context and b) a different context.

- match
- shoot
- score
- dribble
- strike
- mark

Find the words in this paragraph that are homonyms.

The draw for the FA Cup can be seen live on TV and online. The first out of the bag will play at home.

Game On

Answer these questions with full sentences.

1. For how long was Graham Hicks a professional footballer?
2. How long will it be before new Academy scholars can get a pro contract?
3. Why does Graham Hicks say he will throw mobiles out of the window?
4. What does Graham Hicks mean by saying, 'Or maybe I mean you *should* worry'?
5. Write a sentence to describe what sort of person you think Graham Hicks is.

Match-day programme

First and last Jim Fearn, Physiotherapist

First thing at work? The players start arriving at about nine at the training ground, so if I want to get paperwork done, order any equipment or see any reps, than it has to be before then. Lucky I don't mind getting up early in the morning!

Last thing at work? I'll have lads in for treatment till quite late in the afternoon. I go out running or work in the gym with players who are doing rehab. Some days, they just don't seem to want to go home. The physio's room is like the Shelby Town social club. But I don't mind that. They're a good bunch. It's the best laugh in the world. And you get all the football gossip! I have to clean everything down and put stuff away before I lock up at night, though, whatever time that is.

First minute of the game? I remember one afternoon when Barnsley were down here and had a lad sent off first tackle of the game. We hadn't even sat down on our bench! He went mad. So did his manager. The gaffer sent me down the tunnel just to check he wasn't taking it out on the dressing rooms. That was some way to start a game. Mind you, I think they nicked a draw off us anyway!

Last minute of the game? No question about that one. The penalty shootout at the play-off final. Dave Morgan stuck his spot kick in and Wembley – well, the Shelby end of it, anyway! – went absolutely crazy. Fantastic day.

First advice you were given? Well, as far as work goes, it would be Jim Walker. He was the Aston Villa physio and I must have driven him mad when I first started, ringing up asking questions. He told me to listen to the player. If he says he can't move then don't try to move him! What Jim really meant, though, was that every player's different and you need to read him right to get him back playing as quick as you can.

Last advice you gave out? To Dotun Odegbame, the other day. He's still a bit bothered with pain in his shoulder from last season. I said to him, 'Dotun, if it hurts, just have a lie down.' Hour and a half later, I came back and he was fast asleep on my treatment table!

Shelby **STFC** Town

Jim Fearn
Physiotherapist

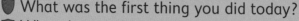

Team Talk: 🛡 What was the first thing you did today?
🛡 What do you think the last thing you do today will be?

Skills Practice 1

Choose the best word you can to join the clauses.

a) They're a good bunch _____ it's the best laugh in the world.

b) We hadn't even sat down on our bench _____ he went mad.

c) The physio's room is like the Shelby Town social club _____ I don't mind that.

d) I have to arrive early _____ the players start arriving at nine a.m.

Skills Practice 2

Choose different connectives to link these pairs of sentences.

a) The job of physio is hard work. It is very rewarding.

b) The physio's room is not very big. There always seems to be room for another player.

Add the best connective to this sentence.

United could have scored more _____ the manager was happy enough to scrape a win.

> **Manager's Message**
> Useful connectives to link ideas are *nevertheless*, *although*, *even so*, *despite*.

Game On

Answer these questions with full sentences.

1. What does the physiotherapist do before the players arrive at the ground?
2. What does the physio do before he locks up at night?
3. What did the physio have to check on when the Barnsley player was sent off in the first minute?
4. Explain the phrase 'you need to read him right'.
5. How do you think the physio reacted to Dotun falling asleep, and why?

Match-day programme

Reserves and youths in focus

Every match day, we bring you news from behind the scenes at Shelby Town. This season, we have a new feature, 'Reserves and youths in focus'. We're kicking off the series today by talking to the man responsible for getting players ready for Mick Diamond's first team, reserve team manager Tommy Fulton.

Not many men find out about a new job standing on top of the roof at a new school! After retiring as a player, Tommy Fulton set up in business as a roofing contractor in Leicester, where City had been his last club. When the phone call came through from former Mansfield team-mate Mick Diamond, Tommy didn't think twice:

'I was at the point where I never wanted to climb another bit of scaffold!' he laughs. 'I was just waiting for an excuse to pack that lark in! My son took over the business and is doing very well. I won't get rich as a reserve team manager but I'd probably pay to stay involved with football, to be honest. I've done all my coaching badges now and I'm really enjoying it. It's a good time to be at Shelby Town.'

Tommy's one of the unsung heroes at Manor Park. While the first team's busy in the Premier League, he's working in much less glamorous surroundings:

'It's a funny situation with the reserves,' he admits. 'I've got the kids, plus lads who are coming back from injury, squad players who need a run-out and first-teamers who've been dropped and aren't too happy about it! I never know what kind of team I'll have from one week to the next!'

Just at the moment, though, Tommy's enjoying working with a promising group of young pros at Manor Park:

'Maybe it's because so many of them have been together for a while now. Half this team were in our FA Youth Cup sides last season and the season before. We're playing more experienced teams and the lads are challenged by that. What they've got, though, is a togetherness that you don't often see in reserve team football. If anything, that enthusiasm rubs off on the older players. I think the future looks bright. And it might happen sooner than Shelby Town supporters expect!'

Shelby STFC **Town**

Tommy Fulton
Reserve Team Manager

Team Talk:

🛡 Why do you think the younger players' enthusiasm rubs off on the older players?

🛡 What makes you feel enthusiastic?

Skills Practice 1

Write your own definition of these words, and then use a dictionary to check them.

a) manager
b) reserve
c) scaffold
d) unsung
e) glamorous
f) promising

Skills Practice 2

Practise spelling these groups of words using Look Say Cover Write Check.

a) feature   season   league
b) series   premier   experienced
c) retiring   surrounding   promising

Identify any words in the following sentence that might be hard to spell and practise spelling them.

Every Premier League club devotes vast resources in striving to uncover the next big-name player, using increasingly sophisticated youth training programmes.

Game On

Answer these questions with full sentences.

1. What was Tommy Fulton's job before he became a roofing contractor?
2. What happened to his business when Tommy joined Shelby Town?
3. What are the qualifications that Tommy has completed for his job as reserve team manager?
4. Why doesn't Tommy know what sort of team he will be managing?
5. In what ways might the surroundings of the reserves be less glamorous than those of the first team?

Shelby Town FC

Shelby Town FC
24 Balcolm Drive
Shelby
Leeside

FAO All journalists and broadcasters

Welcome to another season of Premier League football at Manor Park. In case we haven't met before, I should introduce myself. My name is Sandy Lane and I'm the Communications Officer for Shelby Town FC. I'm here to help whenever I can.

After graduating from college, I worked for several years on the local Leeside paper, the Shelby Gazette. I then set up my own business advising local companies about media and public relations. During that time, I was also a freelance contributor to several national newspapers and magazines. I joined Shelby Town just over three years ago.

The new season

Obviously, we're all delighted to be playing in the Premier League again this season. I'm aware that there were problems last season, our first ever in the top division. We have made several improvements to our system. Everything should work more smoothly now, starting today!

Shelby STFC **Town**

Sandy Lane
Communications Officer

There is a new dedicated window for press, broadcasters' and photographers' passes. It can be found to the left of the window for players' and guests' tickets. You will be expected to produce your Premier League ID card at all times when you are collecting tickets. The club has refurbished our press lounge/interview room and we are now happy to provide refreshments and workstations on match days. You will be able to access the new facilities from three hours before and until two hours after home games.

As you know if you've been to Manor Park before, the press box is difficult to reach from the dressing room area. I will try to ensure that the managers of both teams are available in the interview room within half an hour of the final whistle. Please be patient. If you wish to speak to any of the players after a game, can you try to let us know before kick-off? Thanks again for your cooperation. I hope you enjoy your day at Manor Park!

Sandy Lane

Sandy Lane, Communications Dept, Shelby Town FC

Team Talk:
🛡 What skills do you think a communications officer needs?
🛡 Has your own team ever been written about in a newspaper? What was written about them?

Skills Practice 1

Write a phrase or short sentence to explain the meaning of these phrases.

a) communications officer
b) media and public relations
c) freelance contributor
d) ID card

Skills Practice 2

Write your own definition of the following words and check them in a dictionary.

a) graduation
b) national
c) facilities

d) refurbish
e) workstation
f) cooperation

Practise spelling the above words using Look Say Cover Write Check.

Identify any words you might have difficulty spelling in this sentence and practise them.

Graduates who studied journalism also built up their PR knowledge by studying a module in Sports Public Relations which allowed them to look at the industry from both perspectives.

Game On

Answer these questions with full sentences.

1. Who is the intended audience for the leaflet?
2. For how long has Sandy Lane worked for Shelby Town?
3. What do you understand by the phrase 'dedicated window'?
4. What are the new facilities that Sandy mentions?
5. What problems do you think the Communications department experienced last season?

Match-day programme

Junior supporters' page

Hi, everyone. Welcome to another big Premier League game at Manor Park. It's Diane Eastham here, organiser of the Shelby Town Junior Supporters Club. Hope you're going to have another fantastic day and Town get another fantastic win!

Our mascot today is Wynn Jones. Wynn is seven and attends Leeside Junior School. She has two older brothers. All three of them sit in the family section with their dad on match days. As well as following Shelby Town, Wynn plays netball at school. She loves riding her bike at weekends and building Lego Star Wars models with her brothers. Her favourite player is Dotun Odegbame. Hope you and the family have a great day today, Wynn!

Hello to all our friends from Arsenal's Junior Gunners, especially Dennis Simpson who's the Arsenal mascot today. This will be his first visit to Manor Park. Dennis is nine and plays football for his school, Hungerford School in Islington. As well as football, Dennis likes playing basketball and collecting Top Trumps. His favourite Arsenal player is Robin Van Persie.

Keep your eyes open for the postman next week. The latest Juniors News comes out on Tuesday, with lots of pictures, info, games and quizzes inside. There is a very special free gift inside, too.

We have also done the draw to find out which 50 children will be coming along to Manor Park to meet the players and enjoy our Town Juniors' Christmas party. We will be in touch with the lucky ones. If you miss out, don't worry. There is going to be another chance to meet the stars at the training ground before the end of the season!

And last of all, today's quiz question. The prize is a team photo signed by all the players. The question is: what is the name of Arsenal's manager? If you know the answer, email it to juniors@shelbytown.co.uk. First correct one out of the hat will win that photo!
Good luck and COME ON TOWN!!!!!!!

Shelby STFC **Town**

Diane Eastham
Organiser, Junior Supporters Club

Team Talk: Why do you think this programme page begins, 'Hi'?
What is your favourite team's Junior Supporters Club like?

Skills Practice 1

Change these verbs into nouns by adding a suffix.

a) manage
b) follow
c) support
d) direct
e) collect
f) play

Skills Practice 2

Write the root word of these verbs.

a) going
b) riding
c) collecting
d) coming
e) welcoming
f) introducing

Write the root words of the underlined words in this sentence.

If you are a Junior Gunner and are <u>interested</u> in <u>coming</u> along, send an <u>application</u> with your details.

Game On

Answer these questions with full sentences.

1. Who comes to the matches with Wynn Jones?
2. Who are Shelby Town playing against in this match?
3. How do junior supporters get copies of the Juniors News?
4. Who will the club be 'in touch with' about the Christmas party?
5. How does the tone of this programme page differ from the other programme pages you have read, and why?

Shelby STFC **Town**

Peggy Ellis
Assistant Chef

JOB APPLICATION

Name: Peggy Ellis

Post Applied For: Assistant Chef, training ground

Relevant Experience:

I am 34 years old. I am married with two children who are both at school. I am hoping to go back to work now full-time. I did a degree course in catering at Metro University Leeside. I graduated with honours. I received a special award from the college after I designed and supervised the menu for Speech Day as my special project.

After college, I worked for two years for a freelance catering company, The Meal Deal. We did everything from sandwiches for office meetings through to wedding receptions with silver service for up to 200 guests! What that experience taught me is that there's always a way to make things happen, even when what you're being asked to do looks impossible at first.

I've been away from full-time work for the past six years. Now my daughters are both in school, I want to get back to doing what I'm good at. My husband is a Shelby Town season ticket holder, so I have followed the club's story for ten years now! I have also taken an interest in the new thinking about diet in modern football. I understand the importance of fresh food, balanced nutrition and eating the right things at the right time. I think I could pick up what is needed for our players very quickly if I was given the chance.

I understand from a friend who works on the hospitality side at Manor Park that the staff from the training ground sometimes work at the stadium as well. If this is the case, it isn't a problem for me. I would always be ready to organise childcare arrangements as long as I had 24 hours' notice! What I've got, apart from my skills as a chef, is plenty of enthusiasm for work that I love. I hope that comes across on this form!

Excellent! Please call Peggy in for an interview.
Jane S.

Team Talk: Would you give Peggy the job, and why, or why not?
What food do you eat to keep fit for playing football?

Skills Practice 1

Fill in the missing word to begin the conditional clause in these sentences.

Conditional clauses begin with *if*, *unless*, *provided that*, *as long as*, and *on condition that*.

a) _____ I get this job, I will be delighted.

b) I can work at the stadium _____ I get 24 hours' notice.

c) Peggy will only accept the job _____ the pay is good.

d) We will offer you the job _____ you can provide two good references.

Skills Practice 2

Fill in the missing verbs in these clauses.

a) If footballers _____ paid more, they _____ be very rich.

b) We _____ be on time for the match, provided that we _____ the train.

c) Unless he _____ this penalty, we _____ lose the match.

d) If only he _____ scored, we _____ not have lost.

Choose the best conditional word or phrase to complete this sentence.

United will be fielding a weaker team _____ their star striker is pronounced match fit.

Game On

Answer these questions with full sentences.

1. Where did Peggy Ellis do a degree course?
2. What was the name of the freelance catering company Peggy worked for?
3. What is 'the new thinking about diet in modern football'?
4. Why would Peggy need 24 hours' notice before she could work at the stadium?
5. Write three ways in which Peggy shows she is enthusiastic about the job.

Good afternoon everybody. Hope you've all found somewhere to sit. Today being the start of a new season, I wanted to introduce myself, say hello and set down a few ground rules. My name is Bill Simpson and I'm the Safety Officer at Manor Park. I've been here for several years now. We have good systems in place here but we need the right people to put them into action. People like you! Stewards are very important, even though our supporters don't realise how important.

My background is that I was a fireman for nearly twenty years. If it hadn't been for a bad back injury, I'd probably still be working on the engines now. We had to deal with emergencies on a pretty regular basis. My job here is to avoid emergencies ever happening at all. That's your job, too. In a few minutes, we're going to try a few emergency drills. Obviously I hope we never have to put these into practice. But it's very important that you all know what you need to do in a crisis.

Back in the bad old days, we had to spend a lot of time worrying about trouble in the ground. It's not like that now, thank goodness. Your job now is all about crowd safety. But every now and again, you may find yourself in a difficult situation. Football is a passionate game. And sometimes it gets the better of people, especially if they've had a drink. Always remember that you are supposed to be the calm one. However angry a fan is, make sure you don't get angry back. And if you are having a problem, make sure you call for police back-up as soon as you need it.

Right. If you want to check off your names at the table at the back of the room, we'll go out into the stadium to carry on. It's time for those emergency drills. Then, hopefully, we'll all have time for a cuppa before we open the turnstiles. Thanks for your attention!

Shelby **STFC** Town

Bill Simpson
Safety Officer

Team Talk:

🛡 What problems do you think a match-day steward might have to deal with?

🛡 What do the stewards do at matches you go to watch?

Skills Practice 1

Write your own definition of the following words and then check them with a dictionary.

a) season

b) system

c) regular

d) emergency

e) passionate

f) calm

Skills Practice 2

Practise spelling the following words using Look Say Cover Write Check.

a) basis

b) crisis

c) practice

d) introduce

e) police

f) promise

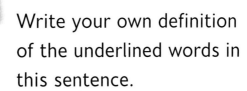

Manager's Message
Try to think of your own way to remember the spelling of similar-sounding letter strings.

Write your own definition of the underlined words in this sentence.

His <u>freak</u> accident is a <u>potential</u> disaster for England and their <u>crucial</u> qualifier.

Game On

Answer these questions with full sentences.

1. Why did Bill Simpson stop being a fireman?
2. What is the main focus of a match-day steward's job?
3. What is the main way Bill's job as Safety Officer differs from his job as a fireman?
4. How has a steward's job changed from the 'bad old days'?
5. Write a sentence describing what you think a safety drill might be.

Shelby Town FC

Shelby Dynamos FC
24 Balcolm Drive
Shelby
Leeside

Shelby Town FC: Doing the business!

You may already be a friend of Shelby Town FC. You may never have visited Manor Park. Either way, I hope you will be impressed by the information and opportunities laid out in the rest of this brochure. I'm Ralph McGregor, the club's new Commercial Director. I hope we're going to meet face to face very soon!

First of all, an introduction. I've joined Shelby Town to bring what we can offer to businesses and individuals up to Premier League standard. My background is in sales and marketing, and hospitality. In the past, I've worked for Hilton Hotels, Audi and the England and Wales Cricket Board. I've never been as excited about a job as I am about the one here at Manor Park!

Shelby Town are a unique club. We're competing in the biggest league in the world. We've got a great team ourselves and, every other week, we're welcoming world-famous clubs and players to the stadium. I want the chance to welcome you too. Come once and I'm convinced you'll be back for more. Why? Because us being in the national limelight doesn't stop us being in touch with our customers closer to home.

In this brochure, we've picked out existing commercial opportunities: executive boxes, sponsorship packages, ground advertising, hospitality facilities. I'm here, though, to make sure we can deliver exactly what you need. Come down to the stadium any time for a coffee and let's talk about how we can do business together. You know your budget and what you hope to achieve with it. I'm here to make sure you spend that budget with us!

Shelby Town are a club committed to excellence. What makes us different is that we're willing to be as flexible as you need us to be. We've got prawn sandwiches if you want them but we can do you balti pies, too! My contact details are on the back cover of the brochure and I look forward to hearing from you very soon.

On and off the pitch, Shelby Town are doing the business! And we want to do business with you!

Shelby STFC **Town**

Ralph McGregor
Commercial Director

Team Talk:

🛡 Why do you think Shelby Town needs a commercial director?

🛡 How does your own team raise money?

Skills Practice 1

Practise spelling the following words using Look Say Cover Write Check.

a) business
b) opportunities
c) commercial
d) committed
e) excellence

Manager's Message
Find your own way to remember where double letters come in words.

Skills Practice 2

Which of these words with the 'ie' letter pattern does not contain the /ee/ sound?

a) facilities
b) friend
c) achieve

Find the words in this sentence with the 'ie' letter string and practise spelling them.

In the Premier League Review we are focusing on the Magpies' belief that their midfielders are world-class players.

Game On

Answer these questions with full sentences.

1. Which three companies did Ralph McGregor work for before he joined Shelby Town?
2. What does Ralph say makes Shelby Town different?
3. What do you understand by the sentence 'Shelby Town are a unique club'?
4. Although Shelby Town are in the national limelight, how do you think they are in touch with customers closer to home?
5. What do you think is the main purpose of this brochure?

Commentator: Minutes till kick-off on BBC Radio Leeside. Shelby Town versus Manchester City is another huge game for Mick Diamond and the boys. It's live, in full and in FM quality, right here. Bill North, our match summariser, is with us at Manor Park as always. Bill – while we're waiting for the teams to emerge, lots of our listeners will remember you as a player at Town. Not so many know you're still involved with the club to this day.

Bill North: Oh, I don't know. I've met a lot of these supporters over the last few years. And even more of their kids!

Commentator: You're now running the Football in the Community department at Manor Park, aren't you?

Bill: Well, my name's on the letters but I don't know about running it. To be fair, I've got some great staff looking after all the paperwork side of things. You know: schedules, health and safety, liaising with schools and youth groups, applying for funding. When it comes to actually going out and doing it, that's where I come in!

Commentator: Doing what, Bill?

Bill: Oh, it's different every day. We go into schools to do football coaching. Now we're trying to tie those sessions in to literacy and numeracy work too, but with all the work based around football. We run soccer schools in the evenings and during the school holidays. We get community groups down to the stadium: senior citizens, disabled groups, unemployed, you name it. Everybody's welcome!

Commentator: And you must enjoy still being part of it all?

Bill: Oh, it's great. It's funny, too. The parents of lots of the kids we work with remember me as a player. The children themselves, though? They know me as – well, the old bald bloke who comes in and does football with them at school!

Commentator: I don't know about the 'old' bit, Bill. But I can't remember you having much hair even when you were a player, to be honest! Anyway, here come the teams. It's Match Day Live, Town versus City, on BBC Radio Leeside.

Shelby **S T F C** Town

Bill North
Organiser, Football in
the Community

Team Talk:

🛡 How do you think having major clubs coaching football in schools helps children?

🛡 Who would you like to coach in your school, and why?

Skills Practice 1

Put the correct punctuation into these sentences.

a) Its live in full and in FM quality right here

b) You know schedules health and safety liaising with schools and youth groups applying for funding

c) We get community groups down to the stadium senior citizens disabled groups unemployed you name it

Game On

Skills Practice 2

Write your own football sentences using each of these punctuation marks.

a) question mark **?**
b) semicolon **;**
c) colon **:**
d) exclamation mark **!**

Add the punctuation to the following sentence.

The Red Devils manager has had a trophy packed career five FA Cups two league cups nine league titles and one Champions League success with the potential to add more trophies to the list

Answer these questions with full sentences.

1. What is Bill North's role with Shelby Town FC?
2. What paperwork has to be done by Bill's staff?
3. Why do you think the football coaching in schools is tied in to literacy and numeracy work?
4. How do you think the children's opinions of Bill might differ from their parents' opinions of him?
5. Why might Shelby Town work at taking football into the community? Give two reasons.

Shelby Town FC

24 Balcolm Drive
Shelby
Leeside

FAO MANAGER

cc PLAYERS, COACHING STAFF, MEDICAL STAFF, SECRETARY

Schedule: Pre-season Fixture, Getafe (A), August 7th KO 7.45pm (8.45pm Local)

Aug 6

15.00 **Coach departs training ground.** All players' kit, staff kit, training equipment, medical supplies etc. to be loaded by Frank Kendall. Players carry on overnight bags etc. which are not to be checked in at airport.

16.30 Arrive **East Midlands Airport.** Priority check-in arranged at British Midland desk. All players' passports and travel documents held by Phil Miles. Depart 17.50/Madrid.

22.00 (Local Time) Arrive **Madrid Barajas.** Immediate coach transfer for players and staff to **Hotel Auditorium, Madrid.** Checked baggage to be transferred to hotel as soon as available (Will Johnson to supervise).

Aug 7

09.00 **Breakfast** available until 10.00.

10.30 Depart hotel for **training session at university training facility.** Details and directions to be advised on the day. (NB We will use local drivers while we are in Spain.)

13.00 **Lunch at training ground canteen.** Menu has already been forwarded and confirmed. Peggy Ellis will supervise arrangements on the day.

13.30 **Return to hotel.** Afternoon at leisure (rooms available, pool, sauna etc. on site).

17.30 **Pre-match meal at hotel.** Followed by team meeting in pre-booked suite.

18.30 **Depart hotel. Travel to stadium (Coliseum Alfonso Pérez).**

20.45 **KO Getafe CF v Shelby Town FC**

For return travel details, please see attached sheet.

Will Johnson

(Travel Manager)

Shelby Town FC

Shelby Town

Will Johnson
Travel Manager

Team Talk:
🛡 What information do you think the 'attached sheet' will contain?
🛡 What would it be like to travel abroad with your team?

Skills Practice 1

Write these incomplete sentences in full.

a) <u>15.00</u> Coach departs training ground.
b) Priority check-in arranged at British Midland desk.
c) <u>09.00</u> Breakfast available until 10.00.
d) <u>18.30</u> Depart hotel.

Skills Practice 2

Rewrite the following sentences in note form.

a) We are all going to meet at the training ground at 8.30 am.
b) Please hand all passports and tickets to the manager before boarding the coach.
c) The team we will be playing against is Real Madrid.
d) After the match we will have a meal with the Mayor and officials.

Rewrite the following in complete sentences.

Man Utd v L'pool. K.O. 6.45 pm

Manager's Message
Think about which words you can leave out and still make sense.

Game On

Answer these questions with full sentences.

1. How long does it take the coach to get to the airport?
2. Which country are Shelby Town going to?
3. Why do you think Will Johnson will be supervising the baggage transfer?
4. Why is Peggy Ellis supervising arrangements for lunch?
5. Write a sentence to explain the purpose of a travel schedule.

Shelby STFC **Town**

Kevin Downing
Assistant Manager

Gerald Sanford: Thanks, Jenny. I'm down at Manor Park for Leeside Sport this evening. Well, where else would I be? Tomorrow's game against Chelsea is the hottest ticket in town. A reminder of how far Shelby Town have come in the past decade. I looked at the record books earlier. On this very day ten years ago, Town were preparing for an away game at Stalybridge Celtic in what is now the Blue Square Conference North. I'm at the club this evening to talk to a man who played in that game and is still at Manor Park now: Town's Assistant Manager, Kevin Downing.

Kevin Downing: Oh, you're making me feel old there! What's worse is I remember the game. We were lucky to nick a 1-1 draw. And I was lucky not to get sent off!

Gerald: And it's Chelsea in the Premier League tomorrow. Do you have to keep pinching yourself, Kevin?

Kevin: To be honest, Gerald, I don't think about it very much, unless a supporter who remembers the old non-league days wants a chat. We just get on with it now, day to day. Maybe it's a bit like riding a bike. If you thought too much about what you were doing, you'd probably fall off!

Gerald: You've seen managers come and go at Manor Park. How are you enjoying the partnership with Mick Diamond?

Kevin: Well, I'm still here, Gerald! Often when a manager comes in, he wants to bring his own people. But when Mick arrived back in 2002, he said he wanted someone around who really knew the club. And that was me. I think it's a good relationship. My job is to concentrate on the players, keeping them fit and happy, so they're ready for what the manager wants us to do on Saturday afternoon.

Gerald: For example?

Kevin: Oh, you know. Nothing too difficult. Just beating Chelsea tomorrow!

Gerald: Kevin. Great to talk to you. Thanks for joining us on Leeside Sport. Don't forget you can hear full commentary from Manor Park tomorrow on BBC Radio Leeside. Match Day Live kicks off at two o'clock. Jenny, back to you.

Team Talk:
🛡 What do you think an assistant manager does to support the team manager?
🛡 Who helps to manage your team and what do they do?

Skills Practice 1

Add the best conditional word or phrase to these sentences.

a) _____ they score in the closing moments, they will lose the game.

b) _____ they score in the last few minutes, we will be the winners.

c) _____ we keep up our defence, we will hold them to a draw.

d) _____ they win away, we will keep our lead in the table.

e) Sixty seconds left, and we look safe, _____ something unlucky happens.

f) You can join our team _____ that you play in goal.

Skills Practice 2

Rearrange these sentences by moving the underlined clauses.

a) I don't think about it very much, <u>unless a supporter who remembers the old non-league days wants a chat</u>.

b) <u>If you thought too much about what you were doing</u>, you'd probably fall off!

c) I wouldn't be here <u>if Mick Diamond hadn't needed someone who knew the club</u>.

Write your own football-related sentence using a conditional phrase: *even if*, *as long as* or *depending on*.

Game On

Answer these questions with full sentences.

1. Who did Shelby Town play against ten years ago?
2. What job does Kevin Downing have?
3. Why do you think Kevin was lucky not to be sent off?
4. When does Kevin talk about the non-league days of Shelby Town?
5. Write a sentence to describe Kevin's relationship with Mick Diamond.

Chairman: So, without further ado, I'm delighted to welcome today's guest speaker at this Leeside Chamber of Commerce luncheon. If any of your children have been running round in Shelby Town replica shirts since Christmas, this is the man responsible! Please welcome our local football club's Retail Operations Director, Mr Tom Wallington.

Tom Wallington: Mr Chairman, ladies and gentlemen, thank you for inviting me today. I must admit I don't do very much by way of public speaking and you're about to find out why! If it's all right with you, I'll say just a few brief words and then I'll be happy to answer questions.

Now, in the old days, I'd have been called a plain old shop manager. That's my background, really. I've never been a great football fan but I was brought up living over my dad's hardware shop in Northampton. I've been working behind the counter ever since, you could say!

When I first went to Manor Park, the whole business was being run out of the club shop. It was successful enough but very small scale. What I've done over the past eight years is slowly to build up the mail order business. You'd be amazed. There are Town fans all over the world who never come to the ground but want to buy stuff for their kids or themselves.

We've got our local supporters, our bread and butter, if you like. They'll only ever spend so much money, though. But if you can be taking orders over the Internet and packaging stuff off, then the sky's the limit. The business we do by mail order and online now is the most important part of the job as far as revenue goes. And that's why I've ended up with a posh title like Retail Operations Director, I suppose!

Now, as I say, I'm happy to take any questions you might have. But I've got to warn you. Don't ask me about football. I don't know anything about it. I'm a Rugby League man, to be honest. On Saturday afternoons I'm usually sat with a cup of coffee, cashing up in the club shop. It's where I feel most at home!

Chairman: Thank you, Tom. Now, who's first with a question?

Shelby STFC **Town**

Tom Wallington
Retail Operations Director

Team Talk: 🛡 Think of a question to ask Tom Wallington.
🛡 What sort of things do you buy from the team you support?

Skills Practice 1

Change the verbs from past tense to past continuous tense.

a) I said a few words.
b) I worked behind the counter.
c) I built up the business.
d) They bought stuff for their kids.
e) They only spent so much money.
f) I took orders over the Internet.

> **Manager's Message**
> Past or present continuous tenses describe actions that haven't been completed, e.g. *He <u>was reading</u> the programme when it blew away in a gust of wind.*

Skills Practice 2

Change these present continuous verbs into simple past-tense verbs, *e.g. I am looking becomes I looked.*

a) I am speaking to the audience.
b) I am selling through mail order.
c) They are listening carefully.
d) They are buying replica kits.
e) We are going to the club shop.
f) Many people are spending money in the club shop.

Change the past-tense verbs in this sentence to the present continuous tense.

Manchester City's star striker has been ruled out of the Cup Final.

Game On

Answer these questions with full sentences.

1. What is Tom Wallington's job?
2. How long has Tom been in the job?
3. How has Tom changed how the club shop sells goods?
4. Why are mail order and the Internet business the most important part of his job?
5. Why do you think Tom feels most at home in the club shop on Saturdays?

Shelby STFC **Town**

Niall Box
Fitness and
Sports Science

Good morning, lads. Hope I'll get a chance to talk to you all individually some time today. The manager thought it would be a good idea to say hello before training this morning. Just so you didn't think a complete stranger had turned up at the club!

My name's Niall Box. I'll leave you to come up with the nicknames. Bet I'll have heard them before, though! Mick Diamond has brought me in to cover two specialist areas at the club, really: fitness coaching and sports science.

I'll take the second of those jobs first, shall I? There are all sorts of different elements that go into getting footballers ready to compete at the highest level: physiology, diet, anaerobic fitness, flexibility, psychology. The idea of sports science is to tie all those different elements up in a bundle. I'm trained to measure what you, as players, are capable of physically and mentally. That gives me the chance to find ways of improving the areas where you might be coming up short.

I can't tell you how to play football, of course; that's the manager's job! What I'm here to do is to try and help you be in the best physical and mental condition possible to do the job you're good at.

You can see that fitness coaching carries on from my work as a sports scientist. You're all fit already, of course. That's why you're doing so well in the Premier League. But Mick has decided that you might benefit from more individual attention.

I'm going to watch training for the next week or so and watch you in games. Then we can sit down and talk, as well. I will draw up a fitness programme for each of you. The idea, again, is to help you get the absolute maximum out of your bodies.

You already have the football ability, I know that. But if we can increase your body's effectiveness by just one or two per cent, I believe it will give you the edge when it comes to winning games.

Thanks for your attention, lads. I think Mick's waiting for you now. Time to go to work!

Team Talk:
🛡 How do you think the players will respond to the appointment of Niall Box?
🛡 Which of the following do you think is most important to your ability as a footballer, and why: physiology, diet, anaerobic fitness, flexibility or psychology?

Skills Practice 1

Write your own definition of these words from the text, then check them with a dictionary.

a) individual
b) specialist
c) physiology
d) psychology
e) maximum
f) effectiveness

Skills Practice 2

Write a new football-related sentence for each of the words in Skills Practice 1.

Write your own football sentence using each of the underlined words.

Portsmouth <u>seized</u> the chance to <u>leapfrog</u> Liverpool in a <u>dramatic</u> comeback.

Game On

Answer these questions with full sentences.

1. Which two areas has Niall Box been brought to Shelby Town for?
2. What will Niall *not* do?
3. How will Niall help to improve the team's performance?
4. Why will he plan a fitness programme for each individual player?
5. What do you think Niall will do immediately after this talk?

http://www.shelby.premiumtv.co.uk/   Google

Logon   Contact A Creative   BBC NEWS | ... Front Page   Demon Inter...Mail: Login   eBay UK – T...Marketplace

Shelby Town FC

Home

News

Manager's page

Fixtures

Match reports

Online shop

Contact us

BE READY FOR THE NEW SEASON – NEW MERCHANDISE RANGES NOW AVAILABLE AT OUR ONLINE SHOP!

Skipper Ready for New Season

With a new Premier League campaign just days away, Sandy Lane sat down with Shelby Town skipper Dave Morgan after training earlier this week. The subject was the one that every Town fan's been talking about. Can last season's heroics be repeated? Can the club establish itself in the hardest league in the world? How does the future look from inside the dressing room at Manor Park?

Sandy Lane: How are you feeling, Dave? Ready for the big kick-off?

Dave Morgan: I'd better be! We've worked really hard this pre-season. The gaffer's brought a new guy in, Niall Box, who's been working on fitness. The bloke's tough on us, I'll tell you! And now I'm 33, you can imagine the stick I get if I don't match up to the other lads. They keep offering to get me a bus pass to use to get to home games!

Sandy: Last season was great for you personally, Dave. You'd waited a long time to play in the Premier League.

Dave: I loved every minute of it. There were ups and downs, obviously. The Carling Cup Final was a fantastic experience for everybody, of course. But the important thing was that we stayed up. Do you know something? Even when we were in the relegation places, I never thought for one minute that we wouldn't survive.

Sandy: What made you so sure?

Dave: Well, I believed in the players. But there was something else. All my time in football, all my time as a Town player, I've never known a team with a spirit as good as ours. And it's not just the team. Everybody at the club is like family, all the people who work at Manor Park behind the scenes. The supporters, too. We're on an adventure together and nobody wants to let anybody else down!

Sandy: Can we do it again?

Dave: Well, the opposition isn't going to get any easier, Sandy! But we can improve and we'll have a proper go at it again. Everybody here believes the Premier League is where Shelby belong!

Shelby Town

Dave Morgan
Team Captain

Team Talk: 🛡 What makes Shelby Town a special club?
🛡 Would you like to play for a team like Shelby Town? Why, or why not?

Skills Practice 1

Rewrite these phrases in full, omitting the apostrophes.

a) I'd better be!

b) We've worked really hard.

c) The gaffer's brought a new guy in.

d) The bloke's tough on us.

e) I'll tell you.

f) I don't match up.

Skills Practice 2

Rewrite these phrases in their shortened form.

a) I would have

b) They would not have

c) They would have

d) They have

e) They had not

f) She might not

Which word in this sentence uses the apostrophe correctly?

We think it's a long time since this club held it's rightful place in the league.

Game On

Answer these questions with full sentences.

1. Who does Dave Morgan mean by 'the gaffer'?

2. What does Dave think was the most important thing about the previous season?

3. Why do the other players offer Dave a bus pass?

4. What do you think Dave means by 'Everybody ... is like family'?

5. Write three reasons why you think Shelby Town will stay in the Premier League.

Here are some examples of the different text types and media in this book. Which ones did you like best? Write your own version of one of these texts in a different style.

▼ Email

▼ Player report

▼ Website

Essay ▶

◀ Interview

◀ Job application

Letter ▶

▲ Programme

▲ Biography